D1265102

THE RISE OF URBAN AMERICA

ADVISORY EDITOR

Richard C. Wade

PROFESSOR OF AMERICAN HISTORY
UNIVERSITY OF CHICAGO

SKETCH
OF THE RESOURCES
OF THE
CITY OF NEW YORK

John Adams Dix

ARNO PRESS

&

The New York Times

NEW YORK · 1970

Reprint Edition 1970 by Arno Press Inc.

Reprinted from a copy in The University of Chicago Library

LC# 79-112538
ISBN 0-405-02447-9

THE RISE OF URBAN AMERICA
ISBN for complete set 0-405-02430-4

Manufactured in the United States of America

SKETCH

OF THE

RESOURCES

OF THE

CITY OF NEW-YORK.

WITH A VIEW OF ITS

MUNICIPAL GOVERNMENT,

POPULATION, &c. &c.

FROM THE FOUNDATION OF THE CITY TO THE DATE OF THE
LATEST STATISTICAL ACCOUNTS

NEW-YORK:

G. & C. CARVILL, BROADWAY.

....
1827.

PREFACE.

—————

In the following brief sketch of a City, the progress of which during the last thirty-five years has been almost without example in the history of society, many material circumstances connected with its general prosperity have been unavoidably omitted. The limits, which the author has assigned to himself, and the want of statistical information have prevented him from giving many subjects even a cursory examination, and rendered it impracticable to enter minutely into the details of any. His aim has, therefore, been to present a general view of the resources of the city, unincumbered, as far as possible without impairing its accuracy, with particular facts.

CONTENTS.

CHAPTER I.

COMMERCIAL ORIGIN AND CHARACTER.

CHAPTER II.

MUNICIPAL GOVERNMENT AND POLICE.

CHAPTER III.

POPULATION AND INTERNAL RESOURCES.

CHAPTER IV.

EXTERNAL RESOURCES.

CHAPTER V.

FUTURE GROWTH ESTIMATED.

APPENDIX.

CHAPTER I.

-->>&<<--

COMMERCIAL ORIGIN AND CHARACTER.

THE origin of every city may be traced either
to commercial or manufacturing interests. It
is the effect of agricultural pursuits, before the
existence of trade and manufactures, to scatter
mankind in a distribution, regulated by attractions
of soil and climate, over the face of the earth.
While the wants of life are supplied by the
direct productions of the soil, and while the
mechanical arts and the business of exchange are
unknown, it results from the regular and irre-
sistible operation of a natural law, that large
cities cannot exist. The condition of society
would furnish neither the elements of their growth
nor of their preservation. It is not until the
mechanical arts are cultivated, and the operations
of traffic and exchange become a part of the
practical system of men, that towns and cities
spring into life, and communicate to society a
new and more complex character.

In extending the view to the growth and progress of cities, it is obvious that their prosperity depends upon the continued operation of the causes, from which they derive their existence. If a city has risen to opulence and greatness from the success of a particular manufacture, it will decline to a certain extent when that manufacture can no longer find a demand in the market. If a city has risen from the success of a particular branch of commerce, it will, in like manner, decline as soon as that branch of commerce is at an end. But a total decline of a city rarely follows the extinction of the cause, in which it has its origin. The accumulation of capital and the divisions of industry, incident to every prosperous city, become secondary principles of preservation, which continue to operate when the original principles, to which we have adverted, have passed away. Thus, a large manufacturing town in the interior of a country may, after the decline of its manufacturing interests, remain important as a depot for the prosecution of inland trade, in consequence of the commercial habits which it has acquired. On the other hand, a commercial town may, after the decline of its trade, continue important from the mechanical arts, which have grown up under the influence and protection of commerce. But this cannot happen where manufacturing pursuits in the one

case, or commercial pursuits in the other, constitute the whole business of the citizens; and the
security of every city from the influence of those
fluctuations, which naturally accompany the progress of society, will be in precise ratio of its
dependance on a variety of interests.

These observations have been deemed necessary, in order to illustrate conclusions, which will
be drawn in the sequel.

The city of New-York had its origin in commercial interests. The first permanent establishment had a view to trade, and was made by the
Dutch West India Company in 1609,* soon after
the discovery of the country, the title to which is
said to have been sold to that Company by
the discoverer, Henry Hudson.† This establishment was forcibly broken up in 1618, by the
English South Virginia Company, who claimed
title on the part of the English government, by
virtue of the discoveries of the Cabots; but the
Dutch were peaceably reinstated in possession, in

* The date of the discovery of Hudson's River, at the mouth of which
the city of New-York is situate, was long disputed, being assigned by some
to the year 1608, and by others to the year 1609 ; but it is now settled
that the discovery was made on the 3d September, 1609. See Chalmers'
Political Annals, Chap. XIX. Yates and Moulton's New-York, Vol. I.
Part I. Sec. 49.

† Chalmers, in the 19th Chapter of his Political Annals, disputes the
sale of the territory, on which New-York now stands, by Hudson, on the
ground that he could not sell it as a discovery, because it was previously
discovered by Cabot, and that he could not sell it on the principle of occu-
pancy, because he had never occupied the land.

1620, by a permission from James I, under which some temporary establishments were made, for the purpose of supplying with water and provisions the vessels engaged in trade between Holland and Brazil. The growing importance of the establishment induced the government of Holland to take it under their protection, and in 1629 a province was erected under the name of the Province of New Netherlands, which retained its form until 1664, when its government was dissolved by Charles II of England, who took forcible possession of the settlement, and transferred it by letters-patent to his brother, the Duke of York, (afterward James II,) from whom it received the name of New-York. In 1673, the country again passed into the hands of the Dutch by conquest, and in 1674 was restored to England by treaty. During all these changes the settlement retained its commercial character and habits.

From this statement of facts connected with the foundation and early history of New-York, it is apparent that the causes, to which its origin is to be traced, have little analogy with those, to which the other settlements of the United States owe their existence. The first settlers of New-England, Pennsylvania, and the Southern States were, with few exceptions, refugees from religious and political persecution, and their abodes in the wilderness were selected—not as fixtures, with a view to the general business of life, but—as asylums to screen them from the oppression, which had expelled them from their homes. These settlements may, therefore, be considered as consecrated by the presence of a great moral principle. The first settlement of New-York was without the benefit of any moral impulse of this nature: her shores were occupied by a commercial company, with a view to trade; and every subsequent addition to her wealth and industry is to be traced to the operation of the same cause.

The records of the city during its colonial dependence are so imperfect, that neither the amount, nor the distribution of her wealth, can be ascertained with precision. But every historical account of her early transactions ascribes them all to the impulse of commercial interests. From some statistical details of the year 1678* it appears that, with a population of less than 3500 souls, she was solely occupied with trade, in which she employed between 15 and 20 vessels of different classes belonging to herself, and rather a less number, the property of the mother country. A similar account of the year 1756 exhibits the same progress from the operation of the same causes.† At this time she was the market for

* Chalmers' Polit. Annals, chap. xix.
† Smith's History of New-York, Part 6, Chap. iii.

Connecticut and New-Jersey, and was extensively engaged in trade with the West-Indies and the mother country. Besides 80,000 barrels of flour, annually shipped to the West-Indies, large quantities of bread-stuffs, fruit, lumber, animals, and salt provisions were exchanged with those islands for rum, sugar, molasses, &c. There was also a considerable trade in logwood with Honduras, and in furs with the mother country. In little more than two months from the 9th Dec. 1755, 12,528 hogsheads of flax-seed were shipped to Ireland. Cotton was also imported in large quantities from St. Thomas and Surinam, for re-exportation to the mother country. Thus it appears that as early as the year 1756, New-York was considered as the mart for the exchange of the agricultural produce of Connecticut and New-Jersey with the manufactures of England; and that a large portion of her commerce consisted in a similar system of exchanges of these manufactures with the natural productions of the West-India islands and the territories bordering on the gulf of Mexico, all of which passed through her as the medium of communication between the commercial parties.

In neither of the accounts above cited is any mention made of manufactures as ministering to her prosperity. The island of Manhattan, on which the city lies, has no facilities for manufac-

turing pursuits, and the great natural advantages of New-Jersey and Connecticut with regard
to manufactures, will for ever confirm the direc
tion, which her capital and industry assumed
from the first stage of her existence. For agricultural industry the island has as little natural
attraction. It is broken and sterile, and this constitutional disability is confirmed by the superior
productiveness of contiguous soils. With these
obstacles in the adjacent country to manufacturing and agricultural industry, and with extraordinary advantages for commerce, it was natural
that the character of the city of New-York should
at a very early day assume a fixedness, with
regard to the nature of her pursuits, from which,
in the whole course of her progress, it has never
for a moment departed. In a subsequent chapter
we shall have occasion to speak of a few manufactures, which have grown up within the city; but
they are such as are independent of natural facilities, and therefore are likely to arise wherever there
are large accumulations of capital and labour.

From the year 1756 to the year 1790 the general progress of the city in population and resources was nearly the same as that of most other
cities in the United States; but from about this
last epoch it was apparent, from the rapid extension of her commercial relations, that she was
destined to take the lead and gradually acquire

3

the character of a general mart for the exchange of foreign and domestic productions. As we shall hereafter see, the causes of her greatness as a trading city are yet but imperfectly developed. She has grown to her present magnitude and importance almost solely by the force of natural advantages; and it will not be until her facilities for artificial communication are fully disclosed, that all the principles of her future prosperity will be brought into operation.

From a review of the foregoing observations and facts, it appears that the establishment of the city of New-York received its impulse from commercial causes; and that she has for more than two centuries maintained a steady pregress from the developement and growth of the particular interests, in which her foundations were laid. It is also apparent from a consideration of her local peculiarities, that she can never flourish by the force of any other interests than those of trade. Manufactures are precluded by physical disabilities. So long as her commercial importance is preserved, her increase in wealth and resources will be rapid and progressive; but a stagnation of her commerce will involve a stagnation of her prosperity, and inevitably lead to the dissolution and decay of that industry, which, by the variety and spirit of its operations, excites and vivifies every section of the country.

CHAPTER II.

———

MUNICIPAL GOVERNMENT AND POLICE.

IN the early constitutions and laws of the provinces and towns of the present United States, framed during their colonial dependance, there are striking points of diversity, arising from the different nature of the sources, in which they had their origin. Those which originated with the sovereign authority of the mother country, are marked with the vigorous spirit of her institutions: those, on the other hand, which grew out of the deliberations of the colonists, are indued with the milder and more cautious temper of democracy. Under the charters of the British kings energetic systems of authority were built up and enforced; while the enactments, fundamental as well as administrative, of the colonial assemblies were carefully guarded against the admission of arbitrary principles. The preservation. for a long time after the establishment of our national independence, of many of the original charters, under which the cities and provinces were first organized, has given an air of incongruity to portions of the local jurisprudence and government of the United States, which would not readily be accounted for by those, who do not trace these diversities back to their source. These monuments of arbitrary rule seem to rise up in the broad field of liberal government in order to mark the career of free principles, and to illustrate the authority of opinion, by the force of which their influence is counteracted and subdued.

The first charter of the city of New-York was granted by James II. and bears date the 22d April 1686, about fourteen months subsequent to the commencement of his reign. The following detail contains some of the principal features of the charter, and is all that is necessary to understand the general scope of its operation.

The corporation was designated by the name of the mayor, aldermen and commonalty of the city of New-York. They were empowered to purchase, hold and dispose of property to the amount of the yearly value of £1000. The royalties of fishing, hunting, fowling and mines (except gold and silver) were granted to them. The mayor, recorder and three or more aldermen and assistants were to compose a common council, with power to make, alter and repeal laws, which were not to remain in force more than three months, unless confirmed by the governor and council. Discretionary fines and amerciaments might be levied by the common council for the violation of their own ordinances: the remedy, by distress and sale of the offender's goods. The mayor and sheriff were to be appointed yearly by the governor and council. The recorder, town-clerk and clerk of the market were to be appointed by the king, or, in default thereof, by the governor or commander in chief. The mayor, recorder, and three or more aldermen, to be justices of the peace for the determination of all matters, civil and criminal, arising within the limits of the city. Aldermen, assistant aldermen and petty constables to be chosen yearly by a majority of votes of the inhabitants of each ward. The mayor to appoint the high constable; and the chamberlain to be chosen by the mayor and three or more of the aldermen with three or more of the assistant aldermen. Mayor, aldermen and commonalty authorized to hold a court of common pleas every Tuesday. They were authorized to lay out streets &c. but not to interfere with vested rights of property, except by consent of the owners.

In 1708, Queen Anne, by letters patent, confirmed the above charter, and granted some further powers, principally relative to the establishment of ferries.

On the 4th Oct. 1732 an act was passed under George II. confirming previous grants of power with some important modifications. The following is an analysis of the charter of the city, as modified by this act, into its principal details.

The city was made a free city. The municipal government to be administered by one mayor, one recorder, seven aldermen, seven assistant aldermen, one sheriff, one coroner, one common clerk, one chamberlain, one high constable, sixteen assessors, seven collectors, sixteen constables, and one marshal. The governor to appoint the mayor, sheriff and coroner annually. The mayor to appoint one of the aldermen his deputy to act in his place in case of sickness, absence or death. Freemen and freeholders to choose the aldermen, assistant aldermen, collectors and constables annually. The mayor and four or more aldermen and assistants to appoint a chamberlain yearly in common council. The mayor to appoint the high constable. The mayor and recorder and four or more aldermen with four or more assistants, to be a common council, with power to make laws, which were to remain in force twelve months from their date and no longer, unless confirmed by the governor and council. The corporation had power to inflict penalties by fines and amerciaments, or by disfranchisement for disobedience of their own laws. The common council had power to lay out streets and make city improvements at their discretion. The mayor, deputy mayor, recorder and aldermen to be justices of the peace with power to hold a court of sessions; to be justices of oyer and terminer and of the goal delivery; to have power to hold a court every week to try all actions, real, personal, and mixed. The mayor, recorder and aldermen to have a several power to try all causes with or without jury, where the thing in demand did not exceed 40 shillings in value. The corporation empowered to purchase, hold and dispose of property to the value of £3000 per annum.

In these different grants of power, it will be perceived that very little essential difference prevails. The manner in which the principal municipal officers were created, was such as to deprive the people of much of their proper influence in the affairs of their own government. From James to Anne, they were for the most part appointed directly by the sovereign; and by the act of George II. they were indirectly appointed by him through the intervention of the provincial authority. The dependance of the corporation was, during the whole of this time, secured by the negative exercised by the governor and council over their enactments. The general mass of municipal power remained nearly the same. The most remarkable point of difference was between the power conferred by the charter of James II. on the common council to make city improvements limited in its operation by rights of private property, and the power conferred by George to make similar improvements without any such limitation. The fiscal powers of the corporation were nominally trebled; but the real increase will be obtained by deducting from the amount of this difference the amount of the diminished value of money from the middle of the seventeenth to the middle of the eighteenth century.*

The following changes by acts of the state legislature and by the constitution of 1821, are modifications of the charter as confirmed by George II. In the view here presented the minor features have not been considered, the object being to give merely a general idea of the municipal powers.

By the act of 9th April, 1813, the city was divided into ten wards. The electors of each ward to choose one alderman, one assistant alderman, two assessors, one collector and two constables. The mayor, recorder, and not less than five aldermen and five assistant aldermen to be a quorum of the common council. A register appointed for registering mortgages, recording deeds, conveyances, &c. Office of the com-

* See IV. Hume's England, Chap. 71st.

mon clerk abolished and clerk of the Common
Council created. Office of Clerk of the market
granted to the corporation. Laws of the Common
Council to remain in force three years, unless en-
acted for a shorter period or unless repealed by
themselves, and renewable at their pleasure; subject, however, to be repealed by the state legislature. Corporation authorized to alter and lay out
streets, &c. and for this purpose, empowered to
take private property upon paying to the owners
the value thereof, to be ascertained by commissioners appointed by the Supreme Court of the State.

The Mayor, Recorder and Aldermen have the
power of police judges, empowered to act as
conservators of the peace.

The Common Council are authorized to pass
and provide for the execution of ordinances
for the prevention and extinction of fires: this
embraces a large class of powers.

The Mayor, Recorder and Aldermen to be
supervisors of the city.

The Corporation to cause sewers to be made,
streets paved and cleansed, and vacant lots filled
in—the expenses to be estimated and assessed by
individuals appointed by themselves.

The Corporation to be commissioners of high-
ways;—authorized to build bridges, make ditches,
construct causeways, &c. to make wells and
pumps, &c. to lay out wharves, piers and slips.

Common Council to make regulations for wharves, piers and slips.—Convicts to be employed at the discretion of the Corporation.

By the seventh section of the fourth article of the constitution of the state, the sheriff, register and clerk of the city and county are to be chosen by the electors once in three years, and as often as vacancies happen. They are removable by the governor at any time within the three years for which they are elected.

By the tenth section of the same article, the mayor is annually chosen by the Common Council.

By the eleventh section of the same article, coroners are elected in the same manner as sheriffs, with the same tenure of office, and subject to the same power of removal.

By the fourteenth section of the same article, the special justices and the assistant justices and their clerks are to be appointed by the Common Council, to hold their offices for four years, unless removed by the county court for causes specially assigned by the judges thereof.

By the sixth section of the fifth article, the recorder holds his office for five years, unless removed by the senate, on the recommendation of the governor.

The charter of the city, as it now stands, is a singular illustration of the changes, which have been wrought in the government of the United States, by their transition from colonial subjection to national independence, and by the general progress of opinion throughout the country. It is a fabric of arbitrary powers, resting upon a popular basis. Almost all the grants of the English kings are retained, and many important additions have been made to the powers of the Corporation by acts of the legislature. But, in confirming and extending the authority of the municipal government, its organization has been subjected to the popular principle of representation, and the citizens have directly or indirectly a voice in the election of most of their officers.

The following instances may serve to illustrate the foregoing remarks:—

In addition to the powers above recited, and many others not mentioned, comprehending almost all the relations, which belong to the business transactions of society, the Corporation have a general power to make city improvements at their discretion, to appropriate to this object private property, upon paying its value, and to tax the property of the citizens to an unlimited extent, in order to carry their plans of improvement into effect.* Under this power, property

---

* The preservation of this power is the more remakable, as in the first charter of the city granted by James II. it was expressly provided, that private property should not be taken by the Corporation but by consent of the owner.

has sometimes been taxed, by the commissioners appointed for that purpose, beyond its value in the market, and the proprietors have offered to surrender the whole subject of taxation, to satisfy the tax assessed upon it. A tax professes to be a sum equal to the rated proportion of a given amount of property; and a tax, which exceeds the whole value of that amount, is without a precedent in any country. These impositions cannot, by any collection of facts or chain of reasoning,

It may be said that the appeal, which lies to the Supreme Court of the State, from the assessments of the commissioners, is a security against the abuse of this power. But the process of redress is often expensive and always troublesome; and it is only in aggravated cases of abuse that it will be resorted to. The case reported in 20 Johnson 430, with others, to which it is unnecessary to refer, indicates the propriety at least of guarding the exercise of this power by additional restrictions. It is not alone in the occasional injury done to individuals that the evil consists, nor in the example of an arbitrary power under a system, which should be popular in its operation as well as in its forms—but it is a universal evil, which, by connecting with the tenure of real estate a liability of this sort, is a positive diminution of its pecuniary value; and in this diminution, every holder of real estate is virtually taxed on account of the insecurity of his possession.

By the law of Massachusetts of 22d February, 1822, incorporating the city of Boston, no other powers are conferred on the Corporation with regard to these objects, than those which belong to the selectmen of the towns throughout the state.

The law of Pennsylvania, 25th March, 1805, regulating the powers of the Corporation of Philadelphia with regard to certain improvements, deprives them of all control over private property. Commissioners are appointed by the Court of Quarter Sessions, on petition, from individuals who are neither residents nor landholders in the city, for the purpose of viewing and laying out the improvement. If their report is confirmed by the court at its next session, other commissioners are appointed in the same manner, and with the same restrictions, to make assessments of damages, &c. &c. and their report is submitted in like manner for confirmation.—By the force of these guards, abuse is utterly precluded.

be made to appear just : they have been submitted to, because they have been made with all the prescribed forms of popular sanction; but they are far more arbitrary and oppressive than many impositions, which, in the absence of these forms, have led to insurrection and revolution in government.

By the fourteenth section of the third article of the state constitution, the special justices and assistant justices are to be appointed by the Corporation, who have also the power of altering their salaries. The pecuniary limits of their judicial authority are such as to give them jurisdiction in almost all cases, in which the Corporation is a party to suits for the recovery of penalties incurred by a violation of the municipal laws. The tribunal to decide these cases between the Corporation and the citizen is, therefore, created by one of the parties to the controversy, and the fundamental rule of natural justice, that no party shall be a judge in his own cause, is violated. This defect in the organization of a judicial authority, which has an immediate control over the persons and property of the citizens, has, perhaps, produced no inconvenience whatever; but in less virtuous times a corrupt influence might be acquired and exercised to the detriment of the public and of individuals; and against the possibility of such abuses it is the business of legislation to guard, by every possible precaution. In fundamental provisions, which are less liable to change than the ordinary legislation of government, these precautions are the more necessary; and in the case under consideration, the limited tenure of office affords facilities for management and influence, which should be counteracted by the conditions of the office itself.

Under the law of 9th April, 1813, a police office is established, and the police judges, (otherwise called special justices,) are authorized to exercise certain powers, which belong to aldermen when out of sessions. By an act of 9th February, 1788, justices of the peace are authorized to commit, for sixty days, any vagrant, disorderly person, &c. on their own view, without a trial by jury. By an act of 3d March, 1820, the term of commitment is extended to six months. Thus, the police justices have the power of taking up and imprisoning any individual at their discretion, without the form of trial by jury. The constitution of the state of New-York* provides for the exercise of this power, by subjecting to trial by jury, those cases only in which that form of trial "has been heretofore used." The powers conferred by previously existing laws are, therefore, confirmed by this

* Article 7th.

specification of cases. This provision is in direct collision with the constitution of the United States,* which declares that "the trial of all crimes, except in cases of impeachment, shall be by jury." That so arbitrary a power has been retained even by legislative provision, and that its exercise has been tolerated by those who are subject to its operation, can only be accounted for by the supposition that it has not been abused, and that the authority of opinion has been such as to restrict it to cases, wherein the rules of justice have been rigidly observed. But a provision, which is defective in principle, is not the less objectionable because it has not been oppressive or tyrannical in practice. The abuse of a system should not only be restrained by the external influence of opinion, but it should be absolutely precluded by the force of provisions inherent in itself.

The time cannot be far distant when these defects in the city government will be remedied. That they will produce any serious inconvenience in the existing state of public opinion is not to be apprehended; but the first stretch of authority beyond the natural limits of that responsibility, which gives a character to all our public institutions, will be the signal for an interposition of the people, and for a total reformation of the

* Section ii, Article 3.

municipal government according to a more popular standard.

It is a remarkable characteristic of an enlightened state of public opinion, though resulting from the operation of obvious principles, that a greater degree of power may be introduced into a frame of government, which has its origin in the people themselves; and that this power may be exercised with less public excitement and discontent, than a similar degree of power under a system, which has its origin in an irresponsible source. In the former case, every measure, which is adopted in pursuance of the constitutional powers of government, is regarded by those, who are subject to its operation, as emanating from themselves; and its inconvenience or severity is mitigated by the consideration, that it is not imposed by any arbitrary interference with their own prerogatives. In the latter case, every act of government, whether arbitrary or otherwise, is viewed as emanating from an illegitimate source, and becomes an object of as much odium as a despotic act committed without any of the forms of popular sanction. Accordingly, it has sometimes happened that a power when exercised under an arbitrary system has produced violent opposition, and, on a reform of government, has been adopted and exercised by the reformers themselves; show-

ing a spirit of hostility less to the substance of
the power, than to the principle in which it has
its origin. To these causes may be traced the
steady existence of a form of government so
arbitrary in its spirit as that of the city of New-
York, while almost every other constitution and
charter in the United States has been so modified as to meet the enlightened character of the
people, and to keep pace with the general march
of opinion. The power of electing their principal officers, and the responsibility thereby secured
to the people themselves, have cast over the
municipal authority an illusion, which would be
immediately dispelled by the adoption of a less
popular mode of providing for its administration.

The police of New-York, with regard to crimes,
is rather remarkable for success in detecting,
than for vigilance in preventing them : scarcely
a crime of any magnitude has been committed
for many years, of which the perpetrators have
eluded detection and punishment.

The police of the city, in the commonly received sense of the term, is perhaps inferior to
that of any northern city in the Union, and has
been the subject of reproachful comparisons by
strangers, who are not familiarly acquainted
with the causes. It will appear by future statements, that the commercial transactions of the
city are equal to all the commerce of the five

other principal cities in the United States; that its population is increasing in a much greater ratio, and that the construction of dwellings, store-houses, &c. is carried on in all the principal streets, to an unparalleled extent. It is the inevitable result of these active and constantly extending operations to crowd the streets with merchandise and the materials of building, and to collect quantities of dirt from the innumerable carts, carriages and animals employed, which even the daily industry of a large body of scavengers cannot altogether remove. That these are the true causes, and that the condition of the principal streets of business is not to be traced to any inattention on the part of the municipal authority to the cleanliness and health of the city, is obvious from the fact, that the streets, in which these causes do not exist, exhibit about the same degree of neatness, which prevails in the best regulated cities in the Union.

CHAPTER III.

———

POPULATION AND INTERNAL RESOURCES.

SECTION I.

THE first statement of the population of New-York on record, is contained in a note appended to the 19th chapter of Chalmers' Political Annals, by which it appears that the number of colonists throughout the province in the year 1678 amounted to 3,430. The manner, in which the enumeration was made, is not stated. It appears also, that the number of dwelling-houses at the same time amounted only to 343. These dwellings could have been, in general, nothing more than cabins, since those of a much later period were extremely rude in construction and limited in dimensions, compared with those of the present day. The proportion of 10 persons to a dwelling was, therefore, very large; but is readily accounted for by a reference to the circumstances peculiar to the condition of youthful settlements in a wild and barbarous region, and in a rude and uncultivated age.

The population of the colony in 1731, according to an authentic computation, amounted to 50,291 souls.

In the year 1755 the whole number of souls in the province was computed at 100,000, and the county of New-York was estimated to contain about one-third of the whole amount of population and resources.* But in the year 1756, according to an official enumeration, by the sheriffs of the several counties, the colony contained only 96,756 persons, 13,542 of which were blacks.†

The first regular enumeration of the inhabitants of the United States, under the authority of the general government, was made in the year 1790, when the population of the city of New-York amounted to 33,131. In the year 1800, the number had increased to 60,489; in 1810, to 96,373; and in 1820, to 123,706. An enumeration was made in the year 1825, under the state authority, by which it appears that the city contained 166,085 souls.

According to the rate of increase from 1790 to 1800, the population of the city would have

---

* Smith's History of New-York, Part VI. Chap. 1st and 2d. The colony of Connecticut at the same time contained above 133,000 inhabitants.

† Spafford's Gazetteer, page 48. In the year 1749 the population of New-York was also estimated at 100,000 souls. Pitkin's Statistical View. Chap. I.

doubled in little more than 12 years. By a reference to the history of the United States, it will appear that this whole period was one of unexampled commercial prosperity. By means of wars and political dissensions, the Old World was making constant and almost unlimited demands upon the industry of the New; our commercial intercourse with Great Britain, the principal trading country of Europe, was established upon the basis of a treaty during the greater part of this period : commercial conventions existed between us and Sweden, Holland, and other trading countries ; and, excepting our differences with France, which were brief in their duration, and at no time seriously prejudicial in their effects, nothing occurred, during this long season of tranquillity, to disturb our citizens in their enterprises abroad. The resources of the city of New-York, which began to assume the character of a general market for the whole country, were brought into full operation by these favouring circumstances, and the increased demand, which arose for men and means, would naturally draw from other quarters the necessary supplies of both. To these causes, and to no other, is to be traced the rapid growth of the city from 1790 to 1800.

According to the rate of increase from 1800 to 1810, the population of the city would have doubled in a little less than seventeen years. It will be remembered, that more than half this period was one of depredation on our commerce by foreign nations, and of restriction by our own government. Captures and condemnations, embargoes and acts of non-intercourse, had so diminished the profits of trade, and rendered commercial operations so precarious, that a large amount of capital was withdrawn from them; and the city of New-York was, as will be seen by a comparison of the rate of increase in population with that of the previous ten years, a principal sufferer from these embarrassments.

The period of ten years, which followed, was one of still greater commercial calamity. From 1810 to 1812, the evils of the preceding period were unmitigated, and from 1812 to 1815, the still greater evils of war were substituted for them. During this time, the foreign commerce of New-York was nearly extinct; and from the entire dependence of the city on commerce, no principle of increase was in operation, by the force of which she could keep pace with the other parts of the United States. From 1815 to 1820, trade again became active, though not uniformly so, and a portion of this period was marked by numerous individual reverses, (the reaction of excessive enterprise) so that the aggregate increase of these last five years, was altogether inadequate to counterbalance the unfavourable results of the five years, which preceded them. Accordingly, it appears from the rate of increase during this period, (1810 to 1820,) that the population of the city would not have doubled in thirty-five years, a rate far below the average progress of population throughout the country. During the same period, population throughout the State of New-York, was increasing at a rate, according to which it would have doubled in about twenty-three years.* The testimony of this fact alone would be conclusive with regard to the position, that the city of New-York has heretofore been altogether dependant on commercial operations with foreign states, and that, these operations being interrupted, there has been no other principle, by the force of which she could maintain an equal progress with other sections of the country.

According to the rate of increase from 1820 to 1825, the population of the city would have doubled in about fourteen years and a half. During this period, commerce was altogether unrestrained, and the rate of increase was about the

* The population of the state of New-York, was in 1810, nine hundred and fifty-nine thousand and forty-nine, and in 1820, one million, three hundred and seventy-two thousand, eight hundred and twelve. While the population of the state was increasing in a ratio of 4.34 per cent. per annum, the population of the city was increasing in a ratio of only 2.63 per cent.

mean of the two highest rates during former
periods. The difference between this period and
the ten years previous to the year 1800, is to
be traced to the decrease of the carrying trade
and to the inferior degree, in which our agricultural, and through it our commercial, industry
was tributary to the demands of Europe and the
dependencies of European states. Their exemp-
tion from wars has left them at liberty, not only
to supply their own wants by the production of
their own industry, but also to carry for themselves whatsoever they produce and export to
supply the wants of other countries.

There is a concurrence in the testimony of all
these facts and circumstances connected with the
progress of New-York, which is so convincing
with regard to the position, which they are
brought to illustrate and sustain, as to render
further comment unnecessary. Assuming then,
the average rate of increase during the several
periods above referred to, as a just basis for an
estimate of the future increase of the city,* its
population in half a century from the year 1825,
will amount to more than a million of souls.

On the accuracy of this calculation, estimates

* In a subsequent chapter the grounds of this estimate will be examined in detail, and an attempt will be made to show that there exists no
sufficient reason to apprehend that the city will be restrained in its growth,
to narrower limits than those of European capitals of the first magnitude.

of the future value of real estate, beyond the present limits of the city, must essentially depend. The whole island would not contain many more than 1,400,000 inhabitants. It is estimated that about one-eighth of the whole surface of the island, including villages, is already occupied. If this distribution were uniform and equal to the greatest density of the city population, the island would not contain more than about 1,300,000 inhabitants; but, on a portion of the eighth now occupied, population is susceptible of greater condensation, and, according to the average proportion of inhabitants to surface in the cities of the United States, it is believed that the final amount of the population of the island will not differ materially from the number first stated. From these data, general estimates may be readily made with regard to the future value of property in lands. For instance, it would follow from these premises that the whole surface of the island, about the year 1780, will be in demand for building lots, and the increase in value of the various portions from year to year will be in ratio of their distance from the present compact part of the city—a ratio diminishing with the approach of population and settlement. The value of particular situations will necessarily be relative to their importance with regard to trade, (foreign or domestic) and that of other situations to their

6

fitness for private residences. These differences are in their nature incapable of being foreseen; but the general result, which has been stated, may be safely relied on as authorized by a fair comparison of the present with the past.*

The population of the city is exceedingly mixed. It was so in its early stages, and new causes have arisen during its progress to confirm and enlarge its prevailing character. The Dutch families, by which the first settlement was formed, are still represented in their descendants, who constitute a considerable portion of the whole number of inhabitants. The descendants of the English families, who established themselves in the province during its colonial dependence on Great Britain, are still more numerous. New-England has furnished a large number of the citizens; and the commercial character of

---

* It is supposed by some, that the extension of the population of the city and its environs, will be nearly uniform in all directions from the present centre of business ; and, as a consequence, that the growth of Brooklyn will postpone, in some degree, the settlement of the island. This supposition might be verified, if the present and future centre of business were to be the same. But it is apparent from the configuration of the island, as well as from recent indications, that the increase of inland trade will bring into use the shore of the North River to a great distance from the southern extremity ; and, if the future extension in this direction is in proportion to the past, the most remote point of the island will, in a very few years, be, with regard to convenience, as near the centre of trade (certainly of inland trade,) as the nearest point of Brooklyn. There can be no cause of apprehension, therefore, that the growth of the city will be retarded, in this manner, to so great a degree as to affect the general accuracy of the foregoing calculations.

the city is such that natives of almost every country in the world may be found in the streets and counting-houses.

SECTION II.

It was intended by the author of this sketch, to give a detailed view of the internal resources of the city; but in making the attempt, obstacles presented themselves at the outset, which seemed to him to be in their nature insuperable. A general result might have been obtained, but not of such a character as to be useful. The only details, which are capable of being reduced to certainty, are connected with the condition of incorporations and regularly organized establishments. All the rest is, in a great degree, the result of loose and uncertain conjecture. The value of dwellings and their appurtenances, of private establishments devoted to the common arts of life, and buildings in general, cannot be determined according to any strictly accurate standard of valuation. Indeed, if an accurate result could be obtained, it is believed on reflection that it would be of no value. Facts of this sort are only useful, when compared with other facts of the same nature. It would be of little importance to know that all the buildings in

New-York of a particular class amounted to a certain sum in value, unless it could be ascertained that all the buildings of the same class in Philadelphia or Boston, according to the same standard of valuation, amounted to another certain sum: and, as will be seen in a subsequent chapter, there is no mode of ascertaining these facts. There are certain kinds of property, which are an index of particular conditions of the public industry, and these it will be our business to consider. But, in the absence of the data necessary to accurate estimates, calculation will be altogether abandoned, with regard to every other species of property.

The amount of capital employed in monied and other institutions, connected with the ordinary business of the city, cannot be taken as a guide in estimating the general amount of wealth. A large portion of the capital (about four-fifths of the whole amount) of the insurance companies consists in bonds and mortgages on real estate. The one, therefore, is but a representative of the other; and, in order to render accurate an individual account of either, the amount of the other would necessarily be deducted from it. But, with regard to calculations connected with the activity of commercial transactions, and the rapid circulation of the subjects of exchange, the amount of capital invested in monied institutions, &c. is undoubtedly a correct guide. It is, perhaps, the best illustration that can be given of the activity of the commercial operations of the city. But it is far from being an accurate measure of the magnitude of those operations. In New-York almost every species of fixed property, by means of hypothecations familiar to the common course of trade, becomes a circulating capital, which is constantly changing its form, and yielding at every conversion a profit to its employers. It is principally in the degree to which this practice prevails, that New-York is distinguished from all the other mercantile towns of the United States. In a city increasing so rapidly in population by the force of external impulses, the extending demand for capital, would render this a natural and almost a necessary resort. From the same cause, considerable investments of capital have been made in New-York by non-residents, so that other cities, and even other countries, by means of these investments, are interested in its prosperity.*

---

* The common notion that the employment of foreign capital is prejudicial to the country in which it is invested, is nearly exploded. The most superficial examination will exhibit a gain, instead of a loss, in every such investment. The interest of this capital goes to the foreign capitalist, but the profits of the industry, which it puts in motion, comprehending the subsistence and compensation of the individuals employed, is obviously a gain to the country, in which the investment is made. The industry of New-York has been in some degree stimulated by contributions of this nature.

The state of the monied institutions of the city, according to the latest account, is as follows:

There are fourteen banks in operation, which are authorized by the laws of the state; and of which the capitals amount to the aggregate sum of $14,750,000. From this amount is to be deducted the sum of $1,150,000, on account of a portion of the capitals of certain companies, which, by the condition of their charters, can appropriate only a part of their funds to banking purposes—leaving a balance of $13,600,000.

The Branch of the Bank of the United States is authorized to employ, in its operations in the city, a portion of the capital of the parent bank equal to $2,500,000.

These two sums amount to $16,100,000, which may be stated as constantly employed in strictly banking operations.

Since the 1st of January the Dry Dock Company has gone into operation with a capital of $200,000 applicable to banking, and $500,000 applicable to other objects.

There are eleven marine insurance companies with capitals amounting to $5,000,000. Four of these companies, with capitals amounting to $1,800,000, made no dividend during the year 1826; two made but one dividend, and one company had not gone fully into operation at the close of the year. The dividend, therefore, accrued on a capital of $3,100,000.

There are thirty-three fire insurance companies, of which the capitals amount to the aggregate sum of $12,450,000. Five of these companies made no dividend during the year 1826, and two new ones, authorized by law, but not in operation at the close of the year, are excluded from this statement. The dividends made by these companies accrued on a capital of $10,300,000.*

The Savings Bank receives deposits to be withdrawn at the option of the depositors. The funds of this institution amounted on the 1st January, 1827, to $1,600,392.

There are several other incorporations, with capitals amounting to the sum of $3,200,000.

The whole amount of the stocks of the city on the 1st January, 1827, may, therefore, be stated at $39,500,392, and this exclusive of the surplus capital and funds of several of the banks and insurance companies.

The increase of stocks since the year 1800, is exhibited in the following statement :

1800,	. . . .	$6,000,000.
1810,	. . . .	11,100.000.
1820,	. . . .	24,100,000.
1827,	. . . .	39,500,392.

---

* For the principal part of the above information relative to the monied institutions of the city, the author is indebted to a view prepared by Mr. T. H. Goddard, published in the Daily Advertiser of the 1st of January, 1827, and politely furnished by the editor of that journal.

Of this last sum, nearly two-thirds has been employed in banking, or in operations connected with foreign commerce; and about 35 of the 39 millions of stock has been employed profitably for the holders. These facts, taken in connexion with the rapid increase of population, are a further illustration of the augmenting resources of the city.

According to a digest of returns of the manufacturing establishments of the United States, prepared under the direction of the Secretary of State, and reported to Congress with the census for the year 1820, the capital invested in manufactures in the city of New-York amounted to $1,780,950. The largest item in the sums which make up this amount, is $300,000, invested in the manufacture of steam engines and castings of every description; the next is the sum of $238,750, invested in refining sugar; and the third, $185,000, invested in the distillation of malt-liquors. All the other sums are comparatively small, and are generally employed in the production of articles of common use and daily consumption within the city.

These details fully sustain the statement made in Chapter I. that the city of New-York has no manufactures, excepting such as are altogether independent of local facilities, and such as are likely to grow up wherever there are large accumulations of men and means.

From 1801 to 1811, the population of the city
of London increased from 900,000 to 1,050,000.
At this rate it would have doubled in sixty years.
During these ten years, according to a statement
in the New Monthly Magazine for February,
1811, there had been annually added to the city
one thousand dwelling-houses. New-York, in
the year 1824, had a population of about 160,000
souls, increasing at a rate, by which it would
have doubled in less than fifteen years. The different proportions being observed in the amount
of population and rates of increase in these two
cases, there should have been added to the city
of New-York seven hundred and ten dwelling-
houses in the year 1824. But it appears from
actual enumeration, by the personal industry
of a private individual, that the number of
new buildings erected in that year amounted
to sixteen hundred and twenty-four. Of these,
at least fourteen hundred were dwelling-houses;
only seventy-six less than the whole number,
which, according to the relative increase of
dwellings and inhabitants in London, will be
annually required, when New-York shall contain twice the present amount of inhabitants,
augmenting at the present rate of increase.
But as the proportion of persons to each dwelling is greater in this calculation than the exist-

ing proportion* throughout the city, it is pro-
bable that the future annual increase of dwellings will be to the annual increase of inhabitants,
as the number erected in 1824 was to the increase
of inhabitants in that year. But the year 1824
was one of great activity—and it is possible that
the new buildings may have exceeded, by a small
number, the average proportion.

* There has been no regular enumeration of the dwelling-houses in
the city for many years. The number was estimated at seventeen thousand, when the population amounted to 100,000,—a proportion of six
persons to a dwelling. But this was mere conjecture, and it is now believed to have been far beyond the real number.

CHAPTER IV.

EXTERNAL RESOURCES.

In the first part of this view, it has been seen that the growth of New-York is owing entirely to the flourishing condition of her commerce. In the last chapter, her internal resources have been briefly surveyed, rather as the evidences of her past and present prosperity, than as the elements of her future growth. The great causes, from which the city is to derive her prosperity and power, lie without; the means, which she has accumulated within, are secondary, and can only be regarded as important, with a view to her future extension, when taken in connexion with the operation of the primary causes, to which we have just adverted. The former are mere materials for the application of industry and enterprise; but the latter furnish, in a large and progressive ratio of increase, both the materials themselves and the powers, which are to assemble and combine them.

We shall now proceed to examine the immediate sources of her future prosperity.

SECTION I.—CANAL NAVIGATION.

The system of internal communication by canals, which the state of New-York adopted a few years ago, and in the execution of which she has made such rapid progress, has given an impulse to the industry of her citizens, of which no foresight can properly estimate the results. A country of vast extent and inexhaustible fertility has been penetrated to its centre, and its productions brought, by the virtual annihilation of distance, which arises from increased facility of transportation, to the very skirts of the city. On the other hand, the productions of foreign countries accumulated within the city by the operations of commerce and exchange, are distributed with the same ease to the various parts of the state, which have become mutually tributary to the wants of each other. It is not within the scope of this examination to consider the beneficial changes, which have been, or are to be, wrought in the social and political condition of the state by the progress of internal communication, or even to ascertain the additions which have been made to the general wealth and resources of the community. Consistently with its design, the system can only be viewed in connexion with the particular interests of the city, and as subordinate to the commercial prosperity, which it is destined so powerfully to stimulate.

From the facts, which have been developed during the progress of the Erie canal, it is clear that its final advantages have been greatly undervalued. The first estimates of the cost of execution fell short of the cost as estimated by the canal commissioners in their report of 1825, by nearly three millions of dollars; but the first estimates of the profits were underrated in a still higher degree. In that report, it was estimated that the canal fund, if properly invested, would, at the end of ten years from 1826, amount to above eight millions of dollars, a sum exceeding the whole of the debt contracted in the execution of the work.* As the principal part of this revenue is derived from the imposition of tolls upon articles transported on the canal, the greater part of which pass through New-York for her own comsumption, for exportation, or for transmission into the interior, it will at once be seen that the commercial industry of the city will receive vast accessions of materials for employment, and that her general increase will be stimulated in proportion. The amount of

---

* See Appendix, A.

tolls for 1826, was $765,104 97 ;* but from the manner in which the tolls are assessed and collected, it is impossible to ascertain the precise value of the articles, on which they are imposed, as may be done in the case of an ad valorem imposition.

If this great channel of communication were limited to the operations of trade within the state, the city of New-York would possess greater sources of wealth, and more abundant materials for commercial enterprise and industry than any other city in the United States. The region of country from Albany to lake Erie, the two extremities of the canal, furnishes more of the elements of human industry than any other region of equal magnitude in any other state. There are, perhaps, sections of country on the western side of the Alleghany mountains, which produce in greater abundance the materials for supporting animal life; but there are none, which yield at the same time so great an amount and so great a variety of natural productions. The

* The annual increase of tolls has been as follows :

1823, ...	$119,988 08.
1824, ...	289,320 58.
1825, ...	566,279 49.
1826, ...	765,104 97.

The amount of the two first years above stated accrued upon transportation on a portion only of the whole line of canal communication. An annual increase may be expected for several years to come, though in a ratio regularly diminishing with the augmentation of the general amount.

salt works of Salina are exhaustless, and distribute throughout the state one of the first necessaries of life, at a rate of cost comparatively of no account. Immense beds of gypsum have been discovered, and are gradually coming into use; and evidences have been given of the presence of mineral treasures of great variety, extent and value, in the mountainous districts of country intersected by the canal. These productions, excepting such a portion as is demanded for the consumption of the interior, will find their way to the city, and add to her wealth by the profits of exchange. The amount in quantity and value of the commodities, which will enter into the inland trade of the state, cannot be calculated upon any data now before the public, in consequence of the uncertain ratio of progress, which a country makes in population and resources, when all the principles of increase are not fairly brought into operation. In countries possessing a full population, skilled in the various pursuits of industry, all further progress will be dependant upon some improvement in the arts, which will furnish means of sustaining upon the same surface a greater amount of animal life. But in new countries, rich in unoccupied lands and natural productions, where the divisions of industry are few and imperfect, and a vast theatre is open for their application, augmentations of wealth arise from the exertion of those natural powers, which are brought into operation by the agency of arts already known to society. So long as there is room for the application of those powers, every addition to the general mass of industry becomes the principle of a further increase, the force of which might be obtained by multiplying the materials and the principle into each other, if the power of each could be ascertained. But in the absence of the data necessary to mathematical precision, speculation must be resorted to, guided in its views by such facts as are in our possession. It was conjectured by Fulton that the number of tons transported upon the canal, in the event of its construction, (which was at the time of his death undetermined,) would amount to 100,000. Others have estimated the final amount, when the full powers of the country are brought into action, at 500,000 tons, without any reference to the extension of commerce beyond the limits of the state. Assuming the last of these estimates to contain the true amount,* augmented by the productions of that portion of the western country, which will hereafter be embraced by this chain of connexion, and it will

---

* This estimate will not be deemed extravagant, when it is stated that the number of tons transported in the year 1826 below the point of junction of the Erie and northern canals amounted to 352,074. As soon as the powers of the country are brought into full operation, an augmentation far beyond the amount of this estimate is to be expected.

be difficult to assign a limit to the influence, which it will exert over the growing fortunes of the city, where these masses of wealth are to be assembled for distribution.

When the practicability of the Erie canal became fully established, and experiment had shown that the profits on the capital employed would be greater than those of ordinary investments, similar improvements were projected in other states. Two canals of great importance to the city of New-York have been marked out, and are already in a train of execution. The first of these is the Ohio canal, intended to unite the waters of the Ohio river with those of lake Erie. This communication may be considered as an extension of the Erie canal, and will render the city of New-York the market for the agricultural productions of a large portion of Ohio, Indiana and Illinois. These states have a surface of 132,780 square miles, are rich in fertility of soil, and furnish in abundance all the materials for manufacturing industry. With these sources of production it is difficult to estimate the increase of trade, which will arise from the diminution of time, expense and labour, by the agency of canal transportation. Few of the productions of these states will stop short of the terminating point of the Erie canal, as the industry of the interior of New-York, being applied to the production of the same articles, both agricultural and manufacturing, the state will be supplied by her own capital and labour, and the proceeds of western industry will find their way to the city of New-York, for the purpose of effecting exchanges with foreign commodities. It is also to be expected from the high manufacturing character of the New-England states, especially Rhode-Island and Connecticut, and the facility with which their productions are introduced into the New-York market, that western manufactures will be for a long course of years effectually excluded, and that this canal will consequently be subservient to agricultural, and not to manufacturing, industry.

It may not be improper in this place to observe that a scheme has been formed of cutting a canal from Albany to Boston, for the purpose of extending to New-England the benefits of the industry and resources of the interior of New-York; and it has been supposed by some that this new communication, by opening another market, would divert from the city of New-York a large portion of the productions of the west, and make Boston the market for the exchange of those productions with importations from foreign countries. But it will appear, upon the slightest examination, that this inference is drawn from a very partial view of the subject. According to the rate of transportation on the Erie canal at the present moment, a barrel of flour may be carried from Utica to Albany (109 miles) for thirty-two cents. Assuming the distance between Albany and Boston to be 170 miles, the expense of transporting a barrel of flour at the same rate would be forty-nine cents. The expense of transportation from Albany to New-York by the freight barges is, according to present rates, only twelve cents; making a difference of thirty-seven cents per barrel, or $3 70 per ton in favour of the New-York market. The calculation, being predicated upon the supposition of an equal rate of freight, is unfavourable to New-York, because the expense of transportation is regulated by the rate of toll, which would, it is supposed, be higher between Albany and Boston than between Albany and Utica, as the country would be penetrated with greater difficulty by a canal communication, and of course a higher rate of imposition would be necessary to defray the expense of the work. But, even according to this calculation, the difference exhibited in favour of the New-York market would inevitably exclude from the Boston market every article produced in the interior of the state of New-York or in the western states, and designed for exportation. It is to be remembered also, that when once a city has acquired an established character as the great commercial emporium of a country, whether from local advantages or fortuitous circumstances, the course of trade becomes settled by flowing regularly in the same channel, permanent investments of capital are made, and the foreign as well as the inland commerce of the country takes a direction, which nothing but the developement of extraordinary superiorities of position in some other place can change. The present superiority of New-York over every other city in point of local facilities for the prosecution of foreign and internal trade is indisputable; and it is only necessary to glance at her physical relations with the different sections of the country, to see that no other position can gain an ascendency over her; for there is no other position, which is endowed with equal advantages. These have already been seen; and, as it is intended in another chapter to extend the view still farther, it will be unnecessary to recapitulate them here. The city, which approaches most nearly to New-York in local facilities for the operations of foreign commerce, is New-Orleans. This city occupies the terminating point of the only natural channel, through which the productions of the south-western states seek a passage to the ocean, and where inland must be exchanged for external navigation. But her advantages of position, with regard to internal communication,

are counteracted in some degree by disadvantages
of climate; and the approach to the city from
the ocean, with all the improvements that art
can devise, will never cease to be inconvenient
and dilatory. The immense power of production,
which the western states possess in fertility of
soil, and in facilities for the application of labour
to manufacturing purposes, is destined to rank
them among the most industrious and productive
sections of the country. But it may be fairly
calculated that the immense regions, which the
Columbus canal will open to lake Erie, including
a large portion of Ohio, Indiana and Illinois,
will become tributary to New-York, from the
greater ease and economy of sending their productions to her, as well as from her superiority
as a market. The vicinity of New-Orleans to
the West-India islands will secure to her a large
portion of the profits of the trade between them
and the western states, and South America will
share largely in her commercial industry. But
on these causes her growth will be almost
entirely dependent. New-York, on the contrary,
besides absorbing the products of a vast interior,
abounding in mineral productions and the fruits
of agricultural and manufacturing industry,
which is already opened to her, will divert as has
been supposed, a large portion of the proceeds
of western capital and labour from its natural

destination, and render it subservient to the enlargement of her own wealth and power.

The Morris canal of New-Jersey, for the execution of which a company has been incorporated by a law of that state, is considered by its projectors as subservient to the interests of manufactures, rather than to the interests of agriculture. The country, which it penetrates, abounds in mineral productions and materials for the fabrics of art; but they are so distributed that a channel of communication is necessary to unite them at a given point, at such an expense, including the cost of manufacture, as will enable them to compete with foreign articles of the same nature. The section of country bordering upon the western extremity of the canal furnishes inexhaustible mines of the Lehigh coal, which will, without doubt, supersede the use of every other species of fuel for household and manufacturing purposes, wherever it can be economically carried. The interior section is rich in iron ore, copper, zinc, manganese, copperas, plumbago, serpentine, marble and lime. The section bordering upon the eastern extremity of the canal abounds in water power, by the agency of which the products of the other sections may be brought into active and useful operation. There is little doubt that the agricultural improvements of the state will be materially aided by the facility of procuring, at a small expense, lime, gypsum, and other manures to assist the natural powers of the soil, and by gaining a less expensive market for its productions, in consequence of the diminished cost of transportation. But it has been supposed that the principal utility of the canal would consist in the power, which it will afford, of bringing into operation the raw materials of an extensive and fruitful region, and of introducing into the markets of the United States, without imposing any tax upon other departments of industry, an abundant supply of many manufactured articles, for which we are now indebted to foreign countries.

This subject is very interesting, especially as connected with the interests of the city of New-York; and as it has been but little discussed, it is proposed, in order to exhibit more fully the advantages, which are likely to result from the canal, to give a separate examination to the state of those productions, which will be brought into activity as the subjects of trade.*

The commodity, which is destined to be of most value to the city, is the Lehigh coal, as a substitute for the fuel now in use for domestic purposes. The rapid growth of the city renders it extremely

* The facts here stated are principally derived from a report of the Commissioners appointed to inquire into the practicability and expediency of the canal under consideration.

desirable that some cheap substitute should be procured to supply the increasing demand, and to prevent that augmentation of price, which always follows an increase of inhabitants, where wood is in common use. Forests are limited in their power of production: a large and increasing population will consume more rapidly than nature can produce; and the demands of an augmenting population upon new lands for agricultural purposes are constantly narrowing the limits, within which the powers of nature are in operation. Old countries have, therefore, of necessity penetrated the bosom of the earth for those supplies, which could no longer be found upon its surface. The importance of coal mines to manufacturing industry is quite as great, as there is no country of full population, where furnaces, if dependent on the productions of the forest, would not yield to such an extension of agriculture as would be necessary to supply its inhabitants with the means of subsistence.

It has been estimated that the consumption of coal in New-York, according to results obtained by an examination of the consumption of European cities in a similar climate, would amount to 115,632 tons; and this exclusively of the coal required for manufactures, steamboats, &c. In this estimate, an allowance has been made for the superiority of the Lehigh over the imported coal in the principle of combustion, the difference being about 100 per cent in favour of the former.* The saving, which this coal would produce to the city, cannot be accurately calculated; wherever it superseded the use of wood, there would be a difference of about 500 per cent.—In superseding the use of Liverpool coal, the difference would be 100 per cent. The latter cannot enter into competition with the former in the American market, for it is well known that it is never imported, excepting as ballast. As merchandise, charged with freight, it would not pay for itself. An estimate of the gain to the city by substituting the Lehigh coal for the fuel now in use, cannot safely be made until the canal is completed; but it may be safely assumed that several hundred thousand dollars will be annually saved, thus creating a new capital to that amount, ready to undergo a profitable investment in some productive department of industry.

The article, next in importance to Lehigh coal, is iron. This article is considered second in importance to the other, because, without its agency, the ores, with which the region intersected by the

---

* This fact has been ascertained by chemical analysis. The writer of this is also authorized by Alderman M'Queen to state, that in the manufacturing processes, to which he has applied it, the result is the same. He has found it equal to a double quantity of imported coal, and he is of the opinion that the iron manufactured by its agency is more valuable in some of its properties.

canal abounds, could not be brought to a laborated state. Of ninety-three forges in the county of Morris, thirty-nine have been suspended in their operations on account of the expense of fuel, which is constantly increasing with the progress of population and agriculture.* The canal, by furnishing an abundant and regular supply of coal at a comparatively cheap rate, will bring these establishments into operation again, and in a very few years it may be safely calculated that the iron of New-Jersey will expel the iron of Europe from the markets of the United States. This calculation proceeds upon the following facts:—1st. The iron of New-Jersey, when well manufactured, is superior in some of its properties to imported iron, without being inferior in any.† 2d. It can be afforded in the New-York market, from which the other sections of the country principally draw their supplies, at a much inferior expense. A ton of Swedish iron commands in New-York about one hundred dollars. It is estimated that the diminished expense of manufac-

* This expense is calculated to absorb two-thirds of the profits of every forge, by compelling the proprietors to keep large tracts of wood-land in the neighbourhood. Thus, for a forge of the value of 5000 dollars, 10,000 dollars must be invested in forest land to keep it supplied with fuel. It is in consequence of these enormous investments that so many of the forges have become extinct.

† The superiority of foreign iron heretofore has arisen from the difference in the European and American processes of manufacture—a difference, which is constantly diminishing with our experience.

ture, from the cheap supply of fuel and the reduced cost of transportation, will enable the iron
of New-Jersey to be sold in the same market for
fifty-five dollars per ton. The diminished cost of
the article, combined with its superior value in
use, must have the effect of banishing the imported
iron from the market, the moment the supply
equals the demand.

The whole amount of iron imported into the
United States in 1822, was $37,077\frac{3}{4}$ tons. At
$90 per ton, which is not far from the average
value, the amount of these importations would
be $3,336,997 50. This amount, as soon as the
market is supplied by the domestic production of
the article, may be invested at home, and will
add so much to the sum of our own industry.

The articles next in value are lime, free-stone
for building, marble for architectural purposes,
and various metallic minerals, which may be
procured at a comparatively small expense and
in exhaustless quantities. The diminished expense, from the increased facility of transportation, will virtually bring all these bounties of
nature to the very wharves of the city, and afford
them in her markets at an expense but little
above that of extracting them from the earth and
preparing them for use. The stimulus, which
will be given to the business of the city by these
additions to the materials of industry, can better

be fancied than explained by any regular train of calculation.

It may be apprehended by some that the growth of the manufactures of New-Jersey will have a tendency to impair the commercial interests of New-York, by withdrawing from employment that portion of her tonnage, which is engaged in the importation of articles to be superseded by domestic production. This apprehension must be limited to the article of iron ; and it may be safely assumed that the general extension of trade in other commodities arising from the causes, which have been investigated. will, even in the first stage of this manufacture, counterbalance any decrease, which may proceed from the home production of that article. The first effect of the success of a domestic manufacture is to banish all foreign articles of the same species from the market. If this manufacture is not forced into existence by arbitrary impositions upon other branches of industry, but grows up with the natural developement of the powers and resources of a country, its success is not limited to this result. It is almost certain, from the economy of labour and expense, arising from improvements in the process of manufacture, to be ultimately produced in such a quantity and at such a cost as will enable it to bear the further expense of exportation for the consumption of foreign countries. This is almost always the case with manufactures, which grow up of themselves, and sometimes with those, which are stimulated in their growth and protected from competition in infancy by the artificial provisions of government. It is in this manner that commerce is indemnified for the sacrifices, which it sometimes makes in favour of other departments of industry.* But in this case, no such decrease of commerce is to be apprehended. The markets of New-York are to be crowded by the productions of one of the richest agricultural and mineral regions in the world. These productions will be exchanged for other commodities, which will be sent to meet them: the materials for commercial operations will be augmented to an incalculably large amount; new capitals will be created and invested in such a manner as to give an impulse to the general business of the society; and, amid this universal augmentation of wealth and industry, it is impossible that any interest can be a sufferer.

From a review of the statements relative to the progress of the several canal communications, which are to have their termination at the city of New-York, and the productive powers, which they are destined to bring into operation, it is apparent that no position in this country, perhaps

* See Appendix, B.

in the world, unites so many facilities for becoming permanently great and prosperous. It
has been seen that the countries, which will
become tributary to her commerce, besides a
fertility of soil not surpassed by that of any
other country, abound in materials for manufacturing industry, and in all the varieties of mineral
production. It remains only to examine the
extent and population of the country, which the
canals will supply, and all the data for an estimate
of so much of her future progress as will proceed
from these causes will have been obtained. It
may be fairly calculated that two-thirds of the
inhabitants of those states, which communicate
with the ocean by the Erie canal, will derive
their supplies of merchandise from the city of
New-York, and remit to her, in discharge of the
debt, the productions of their industry to the
same amount in value. The surface, over which
this population is spread, upon the hypothesis of
an equal distribution, will be as follows:—

Square miles.

New-York, (two-thirds of her surface) 30,800
Ohio, - - - do. - - 25,900
Indiana, - - - do. - - 23,200
Illinois, - - - do. - - 39,420
Territory of Michigan, do. - - 36,000

Total, 155,320

The population, according to the census of 1820, will be as follows:

New-York, (two-thirds of the amount) 915,808.

Ohio, - - - do. - -	387,622
Indiana, - - - do. - -	98,118
Illinois, - - - do. - -	36,807
Territory of Michigan, do. - -	5,930

1,444,285

Thus it is seen, that the industry of a population of 1,444,285 souls will be made subservient by a single line of communication to the commercial interests of the city, and that a country of 155,320 square miles in extent, rich, as we have seen, in every variety of production, will pour its treasures into her bosom, and draw from her the same amount of value in return. To the results of this calculation, are to be added the population and extent of the country opened by the Morris canal, which will, at the smallest possible estimate, be equal to one half of the population and surface of the state of New-Jersey, and we shall obtain the sum of 1,583,072 inhabitants, and 159,480 square miles of country rendered dependent by canal navigation upon the commercial transactions of a single city. In this final sum, it is to be recollected that the last addition contains a larger portion of the manufacturing principle in the natural powers of the soil and in the character of its productions than any section of equal magnitude in the United States. It is also to be recollected, that a large portion of the state of Vermont, which is supplied by the northern canal, is excluded from this estimate, although it might fairly be brought in to swell the amount. As it is, the exclusion of this region of country may serve, if necessary, to counteract any supposed exaggeration in the data, from which the results, above presented, have been drawn.

SECTION II.—FOREIGN TRADE.

From the foregoing examination it is apparent that the inland trade of New-York is yet in its infancy. Until within a very few years, the communications of the city with the interior have been made by the navigation of natural channels, and by land transportation from the points, at which those natural channels have terminated. The great system of internal communication, from which vast streams of wealth and power are destined to flow, has been briefly sketched; and we shall now proceed to the examination of that portion of her commercial resources, which the city employs in her communications with foreign states. The original foundation of the city in commercial interests.

and her subsequent growth by the force of those interests, have already been examined.

If it were intended to give a detailed view of the condition of the city, with respect to her commercial resources, at different stages of her progress, it would be necessary for this purpose to assume three dates, viz. 1678, 1783, and 1825. The first date terminates a period of about 64 years from the date of the first commercial establishment: the second date terminates a period of 105 years from the first date; and the third date terminates a period of 48 years from the second.

During the first of these periods, the progress of settlement was opposed by the rudeness of the country, the scarcity of its productions from the want of cultivation, the hostility of its original possessors, and the uncertain tenure by which it was held, in consequence of the conflicting claims deduced from successive adventurers in the career of discovery. This first period comprehends only about fourteen years of administration under British regulations, the Dutch having held it, at sufferance or by permission of the British king, from about the time of discovery until 1664.

During the second period, almost all the causes, which were in operation during the first, continued, although in a minor degree; and the progress of the city was farther retarded by

10

sanguinary wars with neighbouring colonies, in which they were involved by the domestic differences and disputes of the mother countries, and by the arbitrary and impolitic measures, which were frequently adopted by the governors of the province, in the direction of its capital and industry. But her connexion throughout these two periods with two countries of vast commercial resources, engaged in trade to every part of the world, gave a stimulus to her progress, which these obstacles could not effectually oppose. That the early growth of New-York was aided by the power of Holland and Great Britain, there is no doubt; but the influence exerted in her behalf was subjected to the principles of the modern doctrine of colonization, by which the mother country is at liberty to appropriate to her own use all the profits of that wealth and industry, of which she has furnished the elements. It was from this cause, more than any other, that the progress of New-York was retarded during the second stage of her history. Oppressive regulations were invented to shackle her trade, and give her industry a direction entirely different from that, which it would have sought in the absence of restriction. These embarrassments were shared in common with all sections of colonial America, which were subject to British rule; and they are so well understood, that it is merely necessary to cite them here as one of the most powerful causes, by which the prosperity of the city of New-York was diminished and postponed. During the latter years of the second period, although in possession of Great Britain, her general condition and progress were nearly the same as those parts of the country, which were not occupied by a hostile force.

During the third period, her progress has been rapid, regular, and unrestrained. As soon as the revolutionary war was at an end, and all commercial restrictions removed, trade became active and spirited, and she began to assume a high commercial character among the great cities of the confederation. But it was not until near 1800 that her commercial advantages were properly estimated, and foreign states began to look to her as the future general mart of the country. The hostilities, in which we have been involved since that period, have had an adverse influence upon her prosperity, especially as her foreign commerce, upon which she has been wholly dependent, was for a time almost completely suspended. But from these temporary suspensions she seems to have emerged with renewed energy and vigour, and she is now advancing in a ratio of increase, which has been but once exceeded, and that but slightly, at any stage of her progress.

To present a full view of the foreign commerce

of the city would require more time and labour than the author of this sketch is at liberty to devote to it; and, if obtained, would swell it beyond its prescribed dimensions. There is scarcely a country, which is not visited by her commercial adventures, or a branch of trade, which she does not share with other nations; and it would be difficult to enter minutely into the detail of these extensive relations. Into an estimate of the external resources of a trading city every thing properly enters, which is exclusively devoted, whether directly or indirectly, to operations carried on abroad. The permanent establishments, which are created with a view to trade, are of this nature; but the precise value of these it will be impossible to ascertain. In estimating the value of real property in the United States there is an insuperable difficulty in procuring results, by which comparisons may be made between different places, in consequence of the absence of direct taxation under the authority of the central government. In most European cities, on the contrary, all such property is subjected to taxation under a general authority; and from the valuation, which is made in order to determine the amount of the imposition, may be obtained the relative, as well as the aggregate amount of value of all the objects, on which impositions are laid. The want of such a general system in the United States, in time of peace, renders it impossible to procure, at stated periods, the statistical information, which is necessary to give an accurate relative view of the progress of one city with another in the accumulation of wealth. The valuations, which are made by particular states, having no common standard, cannot be safely taken as the basis of any comparative view. For these reasons we shall only exhibit the amount of shipping, and, as nearly as possible, the extent of the commercial operations of the city of New-York, without attempting to estimate the value of those fixtures, which are subservient to her trade.

The tonnage of the city on the 31st December, 1824, according to the Custom-house books, was as follows:—

	Tons.	95ths.
Registered tonnage,	128,702	56
Licensed do.	132,443	36
total,	261,145	92

According to the laws of the United States, no vessel can be employed in foreign trade without being registered, and no vessel can be employed in the coasting-trade without being licensed or enrolled. The registered tonnage above stated exhibits, therefore, the amount belonging to the city of New-York, which is engaged in foreign commerce, and the licensed, that portion, which is employed in the coasting-trade. This division is not, perhaps, strictly accurate, as some registered vessels, without surrendering their certificates of registry, are employed by their owners in the coasting trade; but this does not often occur, as registered vessels pay the same amount of duties at every entry, which licensed vessels pay per annum.

From the above statement, it would appear that the tonnage of the city is less than it was in 1810, according to a statement made by Mr. Pitkin,* who estimates it at $268,548 \frac{1}{95}$ tons. To reconcile these inconsistent statements, inquiries have been made at the custom house, the result of which is as follows: The amount stated by Mr. Pitkin included all the tonnage, which had been registered for a number of previous years, making no deduction for the licenses and certificates of registry, which had been surrendered, or for the losses, which had occurred during the three preceding years of depredation on our commerce by foreign powers, and of counteracting restrictions by our own government. The amount stated was, therefore, far above the real amount.

The shipping belonging to the city, engaged in foreign trade, is principally employed with that class of operations, which is strictly commercial

* Statistical View. Chap. XI.

in its nature, and not in the carrying trade. The
latter has been almost entirely conducted by the
shipping of the eastern states; and New-York
has probably at this moment a proportionably less
amount of tonnage employed in that trade than
she ever has had at any period of her history. In
commercial operations strictly her own, she, in
fact, employs a considerable amount of the tonnage of other cities. The faculty of commerce
must not be confounded with the faculty of navigation. The latter is the instrument, by the
agency of which effect is given to the powers of
the former. Commerce rests essentially upon
surplus production: navigation, or the business
of carrying, is entirely independent of production,
and may be carried on by a nation, which has no
sources of productive industry at home. This
distinction is strongly illustrated by the distresses
incident to the late war, and the restrictive systems, by which it was preceded.

The value of the goods imported into the city
in 1824, for which duties were paid at the custom
house, was $37,783,147; and the duties, which
accrued on them, amounted to $11,178,139 39.
The value of her exports during the same period,
was $22,309,362, and the duties on tonnage of
every species was $27,592 60.

The progress of a city or state in wealth and
industry can only be understood by a comparison

of the particular facts, which mark the successive stages of its increase. The real value of a fact connected with such an increase is not properly estimated, until its relative value is disclosed; and for this purpose, we shall bring the statements above presented to the standard of similar statements at earlier stages of our national history.

The amount of tonnage belonging to all the United States in the year 1793, was 489,804 $\frac{86}{95}$ tons, including licensed, enrolled, and registered vessels. It appears, therefore, that the tonnage of the city of New-York in the year 1824, amounted to more than one half as much as all the tonnage of the United States in 1793.

The amount of exports from the United States in the year 1792, was $20,753,098. The amount of exports from the city of New-York in 1824, was greater (as will be seen above) than the amount of exports from the whole country in 1792.

The amount of receipts from the customs in the year 1804, at all the ports in the United States, was $11,098,565 33. So that the duties on foreign merchandise, imported into the city of New-York in 1824, without including tonnage duties, light money, &c. exceeded the whole value of the customs of the United States in 1824.*

* It is not to be inferred from this comparison that the amount of commodities imported into New-York, in 1824, was greater than the whole amount of commodities imported into the United States in 1804. It is to be

The amount of imports into the United States in the year 1795, was $69,756,258. So that the amount of importations into the port of New-York, in the year 1824, was more than half the amount of all the imports into the United States in 1795.

It may not be improper to observe here that, by a reference to the statement of imports and exports of New-York for the year 1824, it will appear that the former exceed the latter in value by the sum of $15,473,885, making a balance to that amount against the city. This unfavourable balance is apparent, and not real, as, notwithstanding the manner of estimating their value, it is well known that a large portion of these imports is destined to other parts of the United States as returns for articles of domestic growth, which have been exported directly from the places of production. In comparing, therefore, the value of the imports and exports of the city, the value of these returns should be subtracted from the value of the former. But, independently of this fact, the different modes of valuing the imports and exports, render all inferences drawn from the apparent amount altogether erroneous. It is pretty generally admitted, that all estimates of

remembered, that there has been a considerable increase in the rate of duties from 1804 to 1824, by the force of which the same amount of duties would accrue upon a smaller amount of merchandise.

11

the commercial prosperity of a nation, which are founded upon the balance of trade, are fallacious. The manner of keeping custom-house books affords a very uncertain criterion of the value, both of the productions, which a country imports, and of those, which it carries abroad; and from these books are drawn the data, upon which an estimate of the balance of trade is founded.* In estimating the trade of one country with another, the excess of importation may be counterbalanced by an excess of exportation to a third; and in estimating the whole commerce of a country with all other nations, the precise amount of loss or gain could be obtained only by ascertaining the exact amount in value of the productions, which are sent abroad, at the place of exportation, and of those, which are received in return, at the place of importation.† In a large commercial country, this value cannot be precisely ascertained. In the custom house books of the United States, the value of imported goods, paying ad valorem duties, is estimated according to the actual cost in the

---

* Inferences drawn from the course of exchange between any two countries are admitted to be futile. Ganihl, a distinguished French writer, in his work on political economy, says, (Book IV. Chap. 9.) that there is no certain and positive mode of estimating the balance of trade in any country.

† The cost of production affords only a ground of inference with regard to the value of commodities; since the true criterion must be, the utility of the commodities parted with, compared with the utility of the objects received in return:

countries, from which they are imported, with the addition of 20 per cent. if brought from the Cape of Good Hope, or any country beyond it, or of 10 per cent. if brought from any other place or country. On the other hand, the exports are valued according to their price at the place, from which they are exported, excluding, of course, the cost of freight and other charges, which accrue upon them before their introduction into the foreign market. In fact, this mode of valuation is such that the real balance ought to be considered the reverse of the apparent balance, so that the gain, which a country effects by a particular branch of foreign commerce, would be exactly equal to the excess of its imports over its exports. But any just mode of valuation, by which the real utility of the objects of exchange to the exchanging parties could be ascertained, will always exhibit a mutual gain; for it is only upon such a basis that any system of traffic can be continued for a length of time. The rapid increase of New-York affords conclusive evidence that her commercial operations have been highly beneficial to her interests, and the constant augmentations of population, capital, and industry, throughout the country in nearly a uniform progression for many years, are the most effectual refutations, which can be given to the popular notion of an unfavourable balance of trade derived from partial and inaccurate data.

The following statement of the actual receipts into the national treasury, on account of customs, during the years 1824 and 1825, at some of the principal ports of the United States, will exhibit the relative importance of New-York as a commercial emporium.*

For the year 1824.

New-York, ...	$8,025,110
Philadelphia, ...	2,932,004
Boston, ...	2,675,148
Baltimore, ...	871,271
Charleston, . . .	719,276
New-Orleans, ...	675,659

For the year 1825.

New-York, . . .	$9,803,397 28
Philadelphia, . . .	3,103,194 22
Boston, ...	2,999,053 14
Baltimore, . . .	906,674 17
Charleston, . . .	669,989 86
New-Orleans, . .	679,066 82

By this statement it appears that the importations into the city of New-York in 1824, exceeded by the sum of $151,752 the whole amount of importations into the five other principal ports of the Union. It also appears, that the importations

---

* For this statement, the author is indebted to the politeness of one of the principal officers of the Treasury department.

into the city in 1825, exceeded by the sum of $1,455,419 37 the whole amount of importations into those ports during the same year. The extraordinary excess of the last year is a fact connected with the growing importance of the city, which cannot be misunderstood; it is not only an index of the consequence she has already gained, but it is also prophetic of her future march to a degree of eminence beyond the most sanguine predictions of the past.

The facts, which have been presented in the foregoing pages, render it almost unnecessary to say that New-York, as a commercial emporium, stands alone among the other cities of the Union. The commerce of the latter has been, especially for the last few years, almost exclusively confined to the exchange of articles, the produce of their own states or of the states in contiguity with them, for foreign productions to supply the wants of the producers of those articles. In other words, every city, excepting New-York, has been a particular emporium, limited in the extent of its operations by local disabilities. This remark applies to Philadelphia, Boston, Baltimore, Charleston and even New-Orleans. None of these cities have ever had the character of a general mart, where the domestic productions of all sections of the country have been collected for exportation, and where the importations from foreign countries have concentrated for general distribution at home. Boston has been the market for New-England, Philadelphia for Pennsylvania and portions of the contiguous states, Baltimore for Maryland, Charleston for South Carolina, and New-Orleans for the country upon the Gulf of Mexico and the Mississippi; and to these limits their respective commercial operations have been restricted. But New-York has acquired with regard to the Union the same relative character, which these markets bear to particular states. The productions of every section of the country are accumulated in her warehouses, and the fruits of foreign industry meet them in her markets for the purposes of exchange. She receives the tobacco of Virginia, the rice of South-Carolina, the sugar of Louisiana, and the cotton of Alabama, and sends them abroad to those countries, whose manufactures are tributary to our agriculture. As a part of the same operation, she receives the products of Europe and the Indies, and distributes them to those sections of the country, from which she has derived the commodities, with which they have been purchased. She may be emphatically called THE GREAT COMMERCIAL EMPORIUM OF THE CONFEDERACY; and when the influence of an established character is considered in connexion with local advantages, which no adversity can destroy, there can be little doubt that she will always retain her ascendency over the other great markets of the country.

CHAPTER V.

FUTURE GROWTH ESTIMATED.

To attempt to predict with precision the progress, which a city or country is destined to make in population and resources, is always a precarious speculation. The omission of any circumstance, which contributes in the slightest degree to the result, necessarily vitiates the estimate; and the constantly varying phases, which are presented by a country of great natural resources in the process of developement, either by means of new connexions abroad, or new improvements at home, are an endless source of doubt and uncertainty with those, who venture to extend their view to the future, in withdrawing it from the past. There are cases, however, where the operation of a cause has been so long and uniformly continued as to justify the belief that it is still to be resorted to, as a principle of steady efficacy, in inferences with regard to the future. Of this nature is the case of New-York, in its dependence on commercial interests, as has been seen in the first and third chapters of this sketch; and if the degree, in which trade is hereafter to remain free or become embarrassed, could be ascertained with precision, the future increase of the city might be predicted with the same certainty.

The facts presented in the first and third chapters establish not only that the city of New-York has been exclusively dependent upon trade, but also upon foreign trade. From 1810 to 1820, internal communication was uninterrupted, the coasting-trade, though occasionally hazardous, was still carried on; and yet, during this period, her population from a previous rate of increase, far above that of the general increase throughout the country, fell down to a rate far below it.

Hereafter, new interests are destined to cooperate with the principle of foreign commerce in stimulating the growth of the city. The great system of canal navigation, which has been cursorily surveyed in the last chapter, makes her the depot for the productions of an immense region of country; and, if foreign trade should be altogether extinguished, she would still remain the medium of communication between the different sections of the Union. The productions of the south and north-west must meet for exchange in her markets, and the amount of these will increase with the extension of manufactures in the north and east—an interest, which, by the force of natural facilities, will eventually overcome all the obstacles opposed to its progress.* It may, therefore, be safely assumed, that if the foreign connexions of the city should, by any future adversity, be cut off, her progress will not be checked to so great a degree as it has been heretofore: her dependence on external trade is no longer exclusive; and she will be sustained, in its absence, by the force of new principles, less efficacious and more restricted in their operation, but which ought at least to enable her to keep pace with the general march of the country in population and resources.

New-York will undergo no change of character by means of these new developements. External may be exchanged for internal trade; but she will still be purely a trading city, and to the principle of commerce her prosperity is hereafter, as at present, to be traced.

It has been common to assume, that the limits of a trading city cannot extend beyond a certain point, from some supposed inefficacy beyond that point in the principle of commerce itself. or on

See Appendix, (C.)

12

account of some physical inconvenience, by which its operations would be restricted to a limited sphere. But in the attempts, which have been made to assign that point, there has been a great want of concurrence. It is also assumed, as a consequence of the former assumption, that London, Paris, and some other European capitals, could not have grown to their present magnitude, but for the presence and patronage of a court; and the principle is applied to the city of New-York with a view to establish that her progress, after attaining a certain point in population and resources, will terminate by an exhaustion of its own force. It is almost unnecessary to say, that these inferences are derived from a very vague conception of the subject. With regard to the great European capitals just referred to, all that can safely be asserted is, that the presence of a court is an additional power, by virtue of which a city may be carried beyond the point, at which, without the influence of that power, its growth would have terminated. But it does not prove, that other cities, under peculiarly favourable circumstances, may not attain an equal degree of wealth and power from the operation of other causes.

It may be laid down as a principle, that the dimensions of a city, which is purely commercial in its character, will be in a compound proportion to the wealth and resources of the country, which it supplies, and to the degree, in which it is tributary to the supply of that country.

Trading cities, both ancient and modern, may all be brought to the test of this principle. If the latter have not grown to the dimensions of other cities not purely commercial, it is because commerce has been restrained by some want of facilities, which it is believed will be readily disclosed by a particular examination of each individual case. There is no trading town in Europe that bears to the country, to which it belongs, the same relation, which New-York bears to the United States. The commercial cities of Europe, with the exception of large capitals, (these are excluded, because their growth is to be traced to a compound influence,) are for the most part tributary as markets to countries of limited means, or tributary in a limited degree to countries of extensive means. The cities of Hamburgh, Lisbon, Genoa, Venice and many others, may be cited as instances, in which the countries supplied are limited in extent and resources, and where the principle of commerce would be restrained by physical disabilities. Amsterdam, Liverpool, Bordeaux and others may be cited as instances, wherein, although the countries supplied are vast in extent or resources, yet, commerce being shared by other cities, their growth would be relative to the degree, in which

they severally participate in it. But even these
cases, upon the most narrow view, would not all
concur in giving strength to the assumption under
examination. Liverpool has grown to a magnitude, and is increasing with a degree of rapidity,
which, taken in connexion with the rivalry of
London and other commercial towns in England,
are conclusive as to its fallacy. The cities of
Manchester and Birmingham have risen, in the
same manner, from the impulse of manufacturing
interests. All of these have been without the
benefit of any of those influences, which are
derived from the presence of royalty. These
cases are only cited to show, that there is but one
rule with regard to the progress of towns—and
that, regulated by the degree in which they are
capable of ministering, by any species of industry,
to the industry of other societies. Apprehensions,
therefore, of the interruption of a commercial
city in the course of its progress, for any other
reason than the common one—that there is no
further demand for the products of its industry—
are derived from a notion, which is defective in
point of reasoning, and equally so in point of
fact.

New-York, as a commercial city, is almost
without restriction of any sort. She has the
character of a general market, which natural
facilities have enabled her to establish. and which

the same facilities will enable her to maintain;
and the country, which requires the aid of her
commercial industry, is, by means of natural
advantages and powers, increasing with a degree
of force, of which no foresight can venture to
assign the limits or estimate the results. It is
fair to infer that her growth will be, in some
degree, relative to the growth of the country, with
which, as we have seen, she is inseparably connected; because, with the increase of the latter
in population and wealth, there must also be an
extension of commerce; and, in ministering to
this, the city will become endowed with enlarged
capacities. When this commerce shall have
attained its utmost limit of extension, it would
follow, from the principle we have constantly kept
in view, that the city will cease to make further
advances, excepting so far as it participates in
that general progress of the country, the influence
of which is communicated in some degree to all
its parts. But the growth of the contiguous or
dependent regions referred to is in itself a very
considerable power to the city, and to comprehend
its importance, it may not be improper to go
into a brief examination, in order to bring it to
the standard of the average rate of increase
throughout the United States since the year 1790.

The population of the United States in the
year 1790 amounted to 3.929.326 souls: in 1800

to 5,309,758; in 1810 to 7,239,903; and in 1820 to 9,625,734. During the first of these periods of ten years, the rate of increase would be 3.51 per cent. per annum, according to which the population of the country would double in about 28 years and a half: during the second period the rate of increase would be 3.63 per cent. according to which it would double in about 27 years and a half; and during the third period the rate of increase would be 3.29 per cent. according to which it would double in 30 years and a third. The average rate of increase during the three periods would be 3.47 per cent. according to which the population of the country would double in about 29 years.*

In Chapter IV it has been seen that a population of 1,444,285 souls in the interior of the country would become dependent by canal navigation upon the city of New-York for those supplies, which are procured by exchange with foreign countries. According to the average rate of increase above stated, the surface, over which this population is spread, would, in the year 1749,

* This rapidity of increase is best illustrated by a single comparison. According to a statement of Mr. Malthus, in his work on population, (Book 2d, Chapter ix,) the highest estimates of the population of England at the close of the eighteenth century, would not make it double in less than 125 years. The rate of increase would only be equal to four-fifths per cent. —a striking contrast with the progress of the United States, and apparently extraordinary, when the great prosperity of that country is considered, although readily explained by difference of circumstances.

contain **2,888,570** souls; and in the year **1878** the number would amount to **5,777,140.** In proportion as new countries become occupied, the rate increase in population is naturally diminished, because the necessaries of life, in proportion to the demand for them, become less abundant, and are procured with a greater amount of labor;* but by referring to the chapter above-mentioned, it will be seen that the portions of country, which will be tributary to the city of New-York, are precisely those, where the highest rate of increase during the last **30** years may be expected to continue, those portions being extremely fertile, rich in the materials for manufacturing industry, and, for the most part, but thinly inhabited. The contiguity or dependence of a region of country, in which population and wealth are rapidly increasing, cannot be without effect; and, in the

---

* This observation is confirmed by the statements above presented. From 1790 to 1800, the population of the country, as has been seen, increased at the rate of 3.51 per cent. From 1800 to 1810, it increased at the rate of 3.63 per cent. but it is to be remembered, that during this period Louisiana was added to the territories of the United States, the population of which, (amounting to 97,401 souls,) according to the census of 1810, being deducted from the whole amount obtained by the enumeration of that year, would reduce the rate of increase to 3.48 per cent.— somewhat below the rate of the previous ten years. From 1810 to 1820, the rate was still lower, being only 3.29 Thus it appears that the rate of increase throughout the United States has been regularly diminishing as settlement has extended and population has become condensed, although certain parts of the country, by means of extraordinary natural facilities, have advanced in a ratio far exceeding the general average.

event of a temporary interruption of commerce with more distant or less dependent regions, this augmentation in the section referred to would have a powerful influence in sustaining the city under the pressure of its embarrassments.

In estimating the future growth of New-York, a measure must be sought in an examination of her past progress, and not in any external view. It would be inaccurate to assume as a standard the average rate of increase throughout the United States: because principles are in operation within the city, the influence of which is felt nowhere else. Nor would it be accurate to take the region of country, which is dependent on her commercial enterprises, and measure the growth of the one by that of the other; because new channels of communication are constantly opening to her new regions of country, external trade is presenting new objects of employment, and the sum of all these is to be added to the influences now in operation in order to determine the rate of her future increase. The true criterion is to be derived from her past progress, modified by the new powers, which have been brought into operation by recent improvements. But, in order that the standard may rather be too low than too high, all consideration of these powers will be discarded and the average rate of her increase from the year **1790*** to the year **1825** will be taken as the basis of the estimate. As this period of **35** years includes five years of great commercial embarrassment, and five years of almost an entire stagnation of trade, the result ought not at least to be considered as exaggerated.

By referring to Chapter **III** it will be seen that the population of the city from **1790** to **1825**, according to four successive enumerations, increased as follows, viz.

From **1790** to **1800**, at the rate of **8.25** per cent. per annum, by the force of which it would have doubled in a little more than twelve years.

From **1800** to **1810**, at the rate of **5.96** per cent. by which it would have doubled in a little less than seventeen years.

From **1810** to **1820**, at the rate of **2.83** per cent. by which it would have doubled in about thirty-five years.

And from **1820** to **1825**, at the rate of **6.86** per cent. by which it would have doubled in about fourteen years and a half.

The average of these four rates of increase

---

* It is only since the adoption of the federal constitution that the growth of any part of the United States has been regulated by principles, which can be considered uniform or fixed. Colonial subjection, revolutionary disorder, or the unsettled condition of the government would render the results of every previous year an inaccurate measure of those, which followed. The estimate is, therefore, founded upon the results of the years subsequent to 1789, at which time the government was organized and went into operation upon the federal plan.

will be 5.97 per cent. according to which the population of the city would double in less than seventeen years.*

According to this rate, then, the population of the city in the year 1842 would amount to above 300,000 souls ; in the year 1859, to above 600,000; and in the year 1876 to above 1,200,000. The estimate made in a preceding chapter, that the population of the city would, in half a century from the year 1825, amount to above a million was not, therefore, overrated.

If there be any, (and doubtless there are,) who may consider this estimate extravagant, it is to be observed in reply to their objections, that in this estimate of the future, the rule has been obtained by a fair comparison of the present with the past. Every estimate with regard to the future is a speculation, and in the very term speculation uncertainty is implied. But he, who derives his standard from the present and the past, is more likely to be right than he, who departs from that standard. If the future does not not conform to it, the variation is occasioned by a contingency.

---

* It would be more strictly accurate and more favourable to an estimate of the future increase of the city, to consider these four periods as a single period of thirty-five years, and to assign to every future period of thirty-five years the same number of duplications, which took place in the former. According to this mode, the population of the city would double in about fifteen years and a half; and this has been the real increase. But here again, as in other cases, the lowest standard has been assumed.

which is in its nature not susceptible of being foretold. But in departing from that standard, there is no other, which can be obtained by any legitimate course of reasoning; because, in abandoning fact, recourse must be had to conjecture; and he, who supposes a variation of one per cent. from it, is as likely to err as he, who supposes a similar variation of 99 per cent. The supposition, therefore, that the city of New-York will never increase beyond its present dimensions, is just as capable of being supported by fact or reasoning, as the supposition, that the rate of increase will be ten or fifty per cent. lower than has been stated, unless it can be established that the influence of some principle now in operation is to be diminished or discontinued.*

In the foregoing estimate of the future increase of New-York no reference has been made to wealth and resources, because there are no certain data for an estimate, with regard to their augmentation. It may, however, be asserted that the proportion, in which population and

---

* In estimating the future increase of the city of New-York the only real ground of difference between different speculators would be in calculating the influence of new or accessary powers. The estimate made above abandons all consideration of such powers, and proceeds upon the lowest rate of increase, according to the most unfavourable standard. A more moderate calculation could not be made upon any imaginable data, and to assume a lower standard would be to convert an estimate founded upon certain principles into one of mere hypothesis.

resources increase, is more uniform in the United
States than elsewhere, in consequence of the absence of large establishments of every kind, and of
great masses of wealth in the hands of a single individual. In a country, where the spirit of society
and the spirit of established political institutions are
both adverse to monopoly, and where it is the regular operation of law to dissolve those accumulations
of wealth, which are the fruit of superior industry
and talents, an increase of wealth necessarily
carries with it a nearly uniform increase of population. Property may be as abundant as in other
countries; but its effects are less apparent,
because it is more diffused. Wherever property
exists in large masses a much greater portion of
it is invested in objects of ostentation and luxury
than in countries, where it exists in a more
uniform distribution. The millions, which in one
country, lie unproductive in the form of a palace
and its vast array of decorations, would in another
take the shape of a thousand productive investments, from the proceeds of which as many families would derive a subsistence. In the former,
increase of wealth does not necessarily involve
increase of population; but in the latter, the one
is a necessary consequence of the other; because
the wealth, which is created, is as rapidly diffused;
and in every such addition to the general mass of

resources is contained the principle of a further increase of inhabitants.* It may, therefore, be stated as a principle, that, so long as the operation of law upon property in the United States is uniform, the multiplication of men and means will bear nearly a regular proportion to each other.

CONCLUSION.

THE investigations, which have been made in this sketch, have not, as was stated in the preface, contemplated any detailed exhibition of the resources of the city of New-York. The limits assigned to it rendered such an object impracticable. It proceeded upon the supposition, that the importance of the city, in its relations with the country at large, was not generally understood, and with the design of presenting the

---

* The truth of this proposition will be obvious upon stating, and examining the grounds of the converse—an increase of population will necessarily involve an increase of wealth. This must take place in countries where property is generally diffused, but it is not necessarily the case, where it is preserved in large masses by the force of law. In the latter, numerous classes of dependants are the usual companions of great capitalists and large establishments; and the common result of the fall of one of these is to consign a whole district to want and suffering. But in the United States, where no such disparities exist, where the accumulations of one generation melt away in the next into the common mass, the absolute dependence of man upon man is almost unknown, and every member of society must necessarily rely upon his little stock of wealth. This condition of property may be expected to continue, so long as we are without a rule of primogeniture and a system of entails, which were cast off with the other badges of our dependence on a regal state.

causes of its prosperity—past, by historical refer
ences, and future, founded upon existing facts—
as briefly as possible.

There is no instance on record, ancient or
modern, of so rapid a growth as this city has had
since its liberation from the embarrassments of
colonial servitude; and it is confidently believed
that its growth will continue undiminished till it
transcends the bounds of every commercial city
in Europe. The minutest circumstance connected with its rise and progress is, therefore,
valuable: and the author will be amply indemnified for the few pains he has taken, if any facts
he has collected, or any suggestion, which he has
ventured to make in the course of his inquiry,
prove of the least use to those, who may have
leisure to give the subject a full examination

APPENDIX.

(A.)

It has been seen by a statement of the Canal Commissioners that the revenue of the canal fund will be adequate to discharge the regular accumulations of interest on the sums loaned to execute the work and, at the end of ten years, to refund the principal of these sums. A new capital will be created, therefore, to the amount of the sums loaned; and a further new capital to the amount of the difference in which the interest of these sums is exceeded by the net profits of the system. Monies applied to purposes of internal improvement, where merely the interest of the sums expended is regularly paid by the profits of the works, in which they are invested, stand precisely on the ground of ordinary investments, unless the improvement affords facilities for the application of the public industry to objects of profit or convenience. In this case it has a value, which is not susceptible of being reduced to numerical precision. But investments, which discharge the interest and ultimately reimburse the principal of the sums employed constitute an increase of capital equal and generally superior to their own amount. To illustrate these observations by applying them to the canal system:—The sums, which are applied to the execution of the work, are a capital withdrawn by the individuals, who loan them to the state, from some productive employment; but, to induce those individuals to make the transfer the profits of that employment must be less or the risks greater than of the employment, which is offered by the state. The act of transfer, is therefore, a gain to the individuals. As soon as the work is completed, a profit is rendered equal to the interest, which the state contracted to pay. As long as the new investment affords the same profit as the old, there can be no pecuniary gain or loss, either to the state or individuals. But the increased industry which the work puts in operation gradually raises the amount of profits above the amount of interest, and the excess goes to the reimbursement of the sums expended in its execution. The process of extinguishment is the more rapid, because, by the force of well-known laws of numbers, every reduction of the principal involves a reduction of the future interest, and the sum of both is the principle of the ratio, upon which the future reduction proceeds. As soon as the sums loaned by the state are reimbursed, the individuals, from whom the loans are obtained, are restored to their previous condition, by being put again in possession of the capitals withdrawn, together with the regular profits on their employment. The state is in possession of the work executed by the agency of those capitals, and here the principal accession of wealth is visible. The state has incurred no expense, the work having paid for itself. That portion of the profits of the work, therefore which equals the interest of all the sums expended on it, represents a capital invested in the work to the amount of all those sums. This is obviously a newly-created capital. The portion of the profits, to which we have just referred, is not in strictness (though in effect it is,) a new capital, but must be considered as reserved from this estimate in the nature of interest on the new capital invested in the work. But the residue of the profits, that is, the excess over the amount of such a portion as is equal to the interest on the sums expended, is also a new capital, a capital constantly increasing in a ratio founded upon the annual excess. These details are very simple so much so, that to some it may seem unnecessary to state them. But they may serve to illustrate the observation—that, if the estimate of the canal commissioners with regard to the extinction of the canal debt be not overrated, (and there is every reason to believe it is not) the effect of the surplus proceeds of that work must be to render the state of New-York more prosperous, and capable of greater achievements in proportion to her numbers, than any nation which now exists.

(B.)

It is not an uncommon argument with manufacturers, that many of the branches of industry, in which they are concerned, suffered immense losses in consequence of the decay of manufacturing establishments at the close of the last war, and, on that account have claims on the other departments of industry for present encouragement. It will appear, upon examination, that, as an argument in favour of any such claim the position is altogether destitute of force inasmuch as the capital invested in domestic manufactures during the late war was principally drawn from the commercial capital, which had been diverted from its accustomed employment by a long course of restriction. That it could have been drawn from no other source will be apparent from a train of very simple reasoning. Before the adoption of the restrictive systems, which preceded the late war, the capital of the country was distributed in a beneficial proportion among the various departments of industry. Commerce and navigation had their share, and so had agriculture and manufactures. The first effect of those restrictive measures was to occasion a total revulsion in commercial industry by altogether arresting its operations. Agriculture was checked to an inferior extent, because the amount of decrease would only be in proportion to the degree, in which it was subservient to the supply of foreign demands ; and even this decrease would soon be compensated by the increased demand of an augmenting population. Manufactures alone, by the diminution of foreign imports, were stimulated in proportion to the decline of the other branches of industry. The operation of these causes upon the capital of the country depends on very obvious principles, and may be seen at a glance. A portion of the capital invested in commerce and navigation, becoming totally unproductive, would immediately seek, wherever the nature of the investment would admit of transfer, new objects of employment. It could not go to agriculture, because the capital employed in that department of industry would already exceed the demand, and a portion of the latter would, for the time, be withdrawn from employment, or the profits on the whole amount would be diminished. The capital withdrawn from

14

commercial operations could, therefore, only procure an investment in manufactures, the capital already employed in the latter
being unequal to the demand for its productions, and of course
yielding a higher rate of profit than any other source of production. Transfers of commercial capital were consequently made
to manufactures ; immense establishments were created at war
prices ; and, on the recurrence of peace, the profits of the capital employed were so reduced from the influx of foreign commodities, that many of these establishments were abandoned, leaving
the whole amount of capital invested a loss to manufacturing,
and also to commercial, industry, from the latter of which it was
originally drawn. This loss might, therefore, as well be de-
plored by commercial men as by manufacturers. It certainly
cannot constitute a claim on the part of the latter for sacrifices
in their favour by any other class of society ; and it is with a
view to establish this position only, that the subject has been
considered. If instances should be brought to counteract this
conclusion, the reply is, that the general reasoning, from which
it is drawn, cannot be confuted by opposing to it the testimony
of particular facts ; for these differ from general principles only
in being derived from a more narrow and limited experience.

(C.)

For several years subsequent to the adoption of the Constitution of the United States, the relations of the country with foreign
states were such that its labour was more beneficially employed
in agriculture than in manufactures. There was an urgent demand in Europe for the products of our agricultural industry ;
and the United States, having the use of more land, in proportion to their population, than any European nation, was not
under the necessity, in supplying that demand, of having
recourse to poorer soils at an increased cost of production.
But the condition of the country now is altogether different.
To have rendered our industry permanently tributary, in the
same proportion with regard to its amount, to the countries of
Europe, it would have been necessary that the foreign demand
for the products of our agriculture should regularly extend in

ratio of the increase of our population. But, while that demand has diminished our increase in numbers has been immense ; and population may be said to have reached a point beyond which every further increase diminishes the relative quantity of our agricultural productions, and stimulates the establishment and growth of domestic manufactures.* The productions of the earth in every country, where there are vacant lands, or a further power of production in cultivated lands, are limited by the demand, and not by the powers of the soil. Where the demand is already supplied agriculture will only be extended to keep pace with an increase of population ; and as the whole labour of this increased population applied to the cultivation of the earth, would yield a greater amount of the articles of subsistence than would be required to supply its own wants the excess of labour would, from the operation of natural laws, seek an employment in commercial or manufacturing industry. This is precisely the condition of the United States ; and, as commercial operations can only be enlarged by an extension of the foreign market for our own productions, the excess of labour, just adverted to, above the amount required to sustain the natural increase of population, will necessarily be applied to the production of those articles of manufacture, which the country demands, and of which it furnishes the materials. From these premises it follows, that every farther increase of population in the United States must diminish the relative amount of agricultural productions, and promote the extension of manufacturing establishments. This fact gives to the latter an advantage over the other divisions of industry, which deserves to be considered in every question affecting them. From the operation of the same causes,

---

* If any occurrence should take place, by which a demand should be created in Europe for the products of our agriculture, manufactures would be in a degree retarded in their growth, and a portion of capital might be diverted from the latter to the former, because there is still a considerable amount of unoccupied land of great fertility, to which recourse can be had without increased expense of cultivation. But such an occurrence is a mere contingency, which is not perhaps likely to take place, and which, if it were, could not be permitted to affect the result of any calculation proceeding upon general principles.

our exports of raw materials, our importations of foreign manufactures and our revenue upon the latter, will increase in a ratio less than population. This result was anticipated and pointed out by Albert Gallatin in a sketch of the finances of the United States as early as the year 1796. And such, in fact, is the natural result of the laws of labour in every country, where there is a rapidly augmenting population and where no artificial causes are brought in to violate their operation.

THE END.